School Days

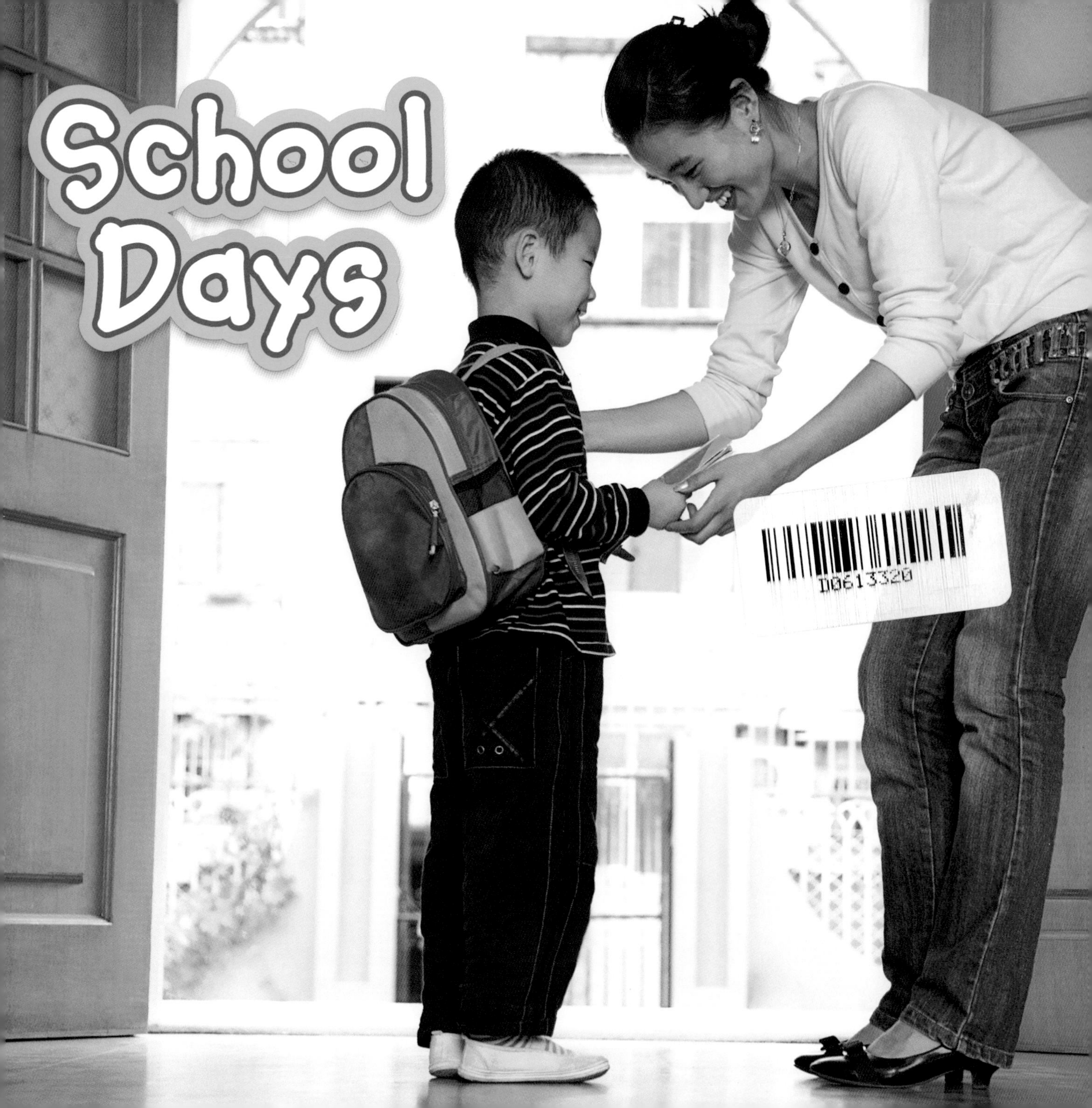

D0613320

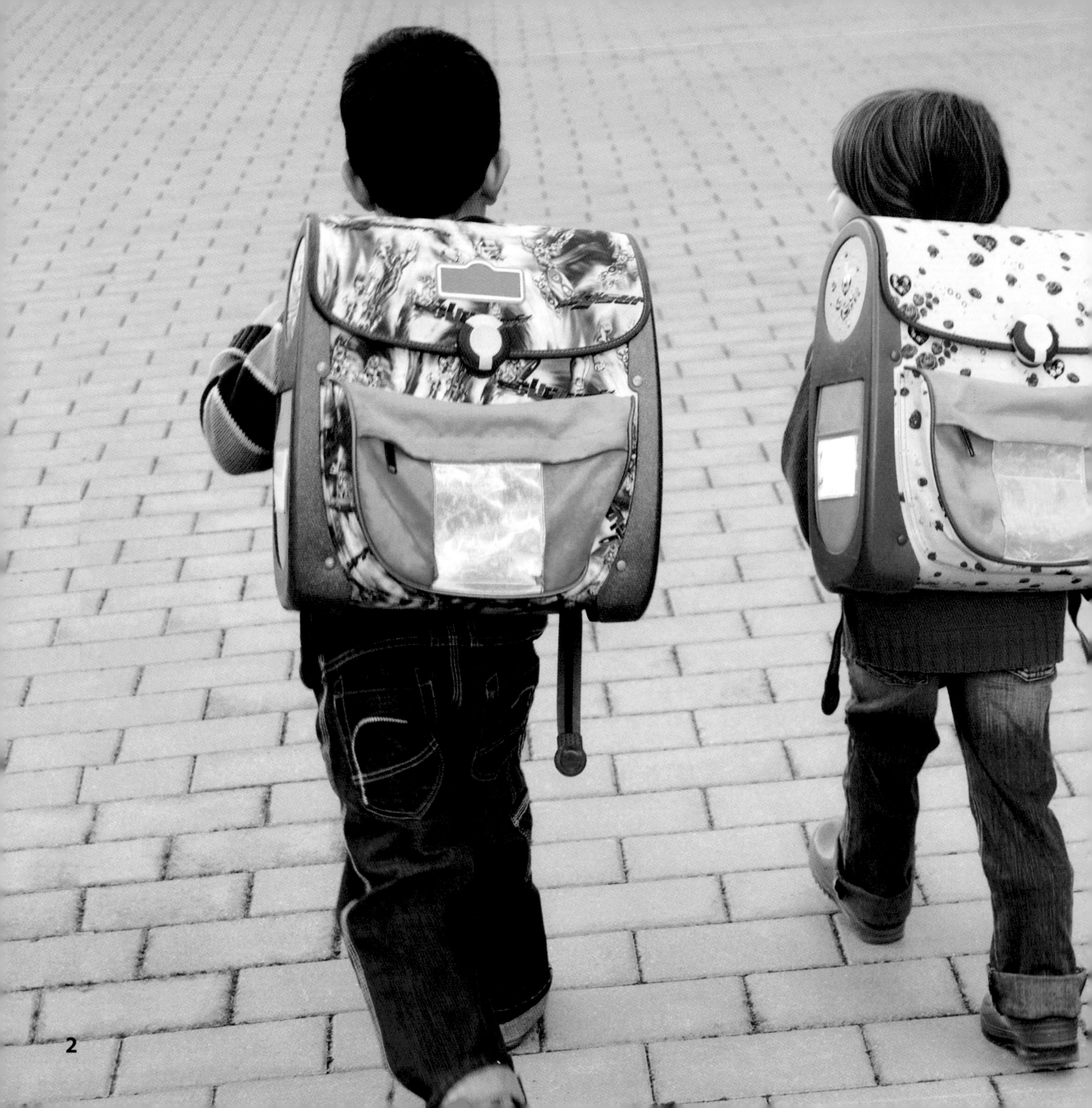

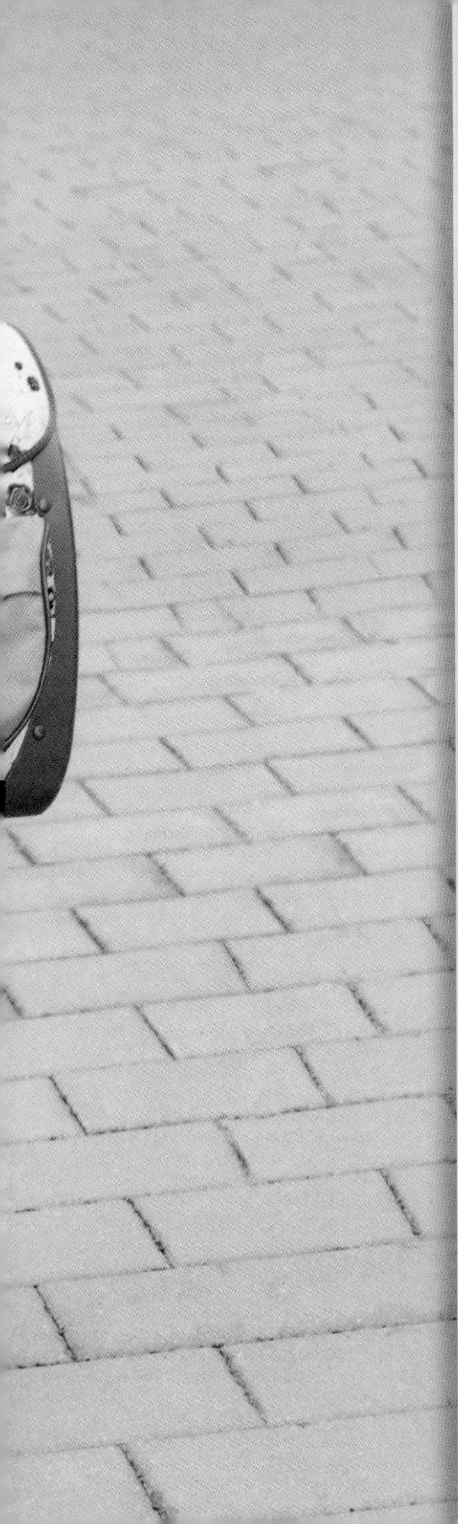

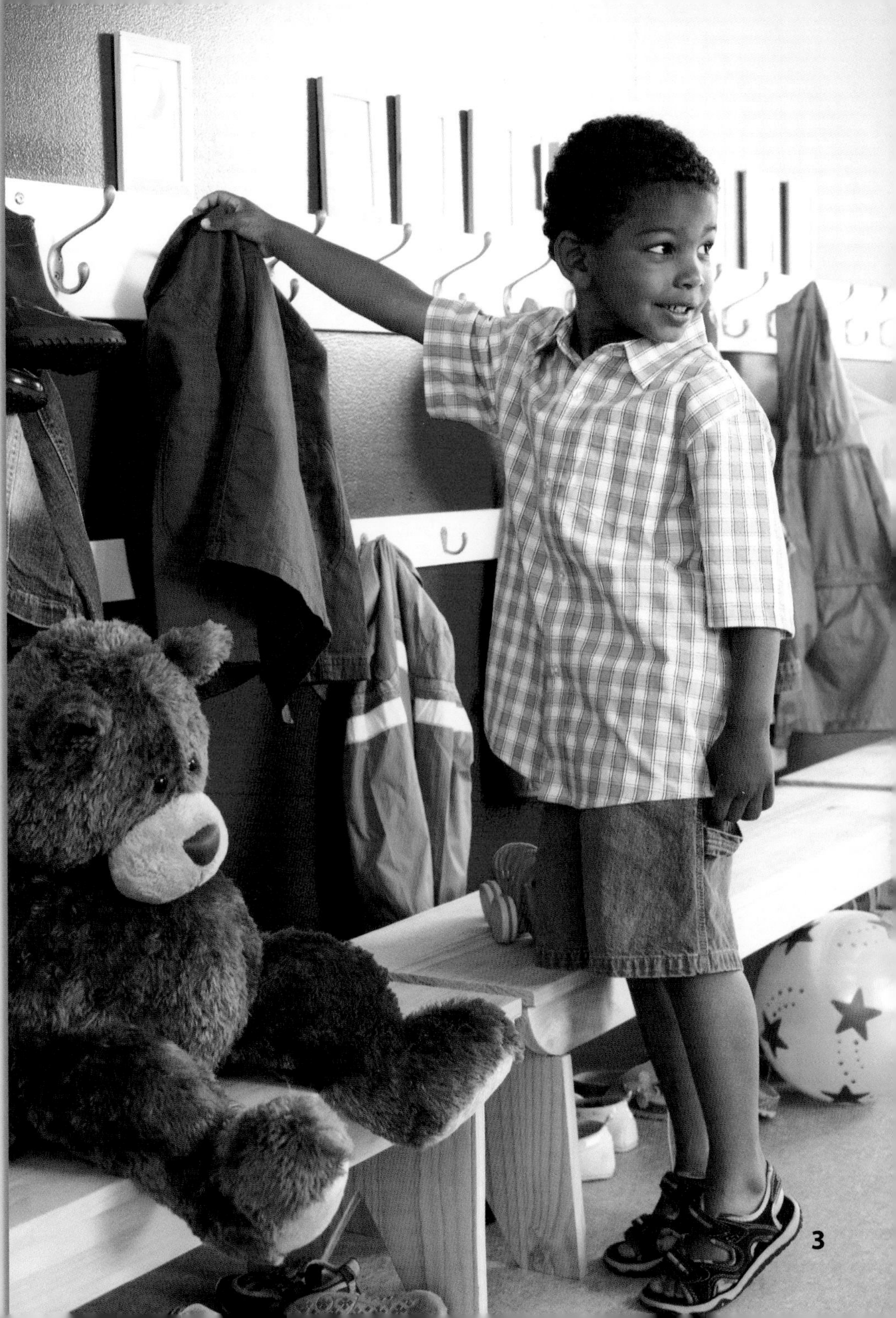

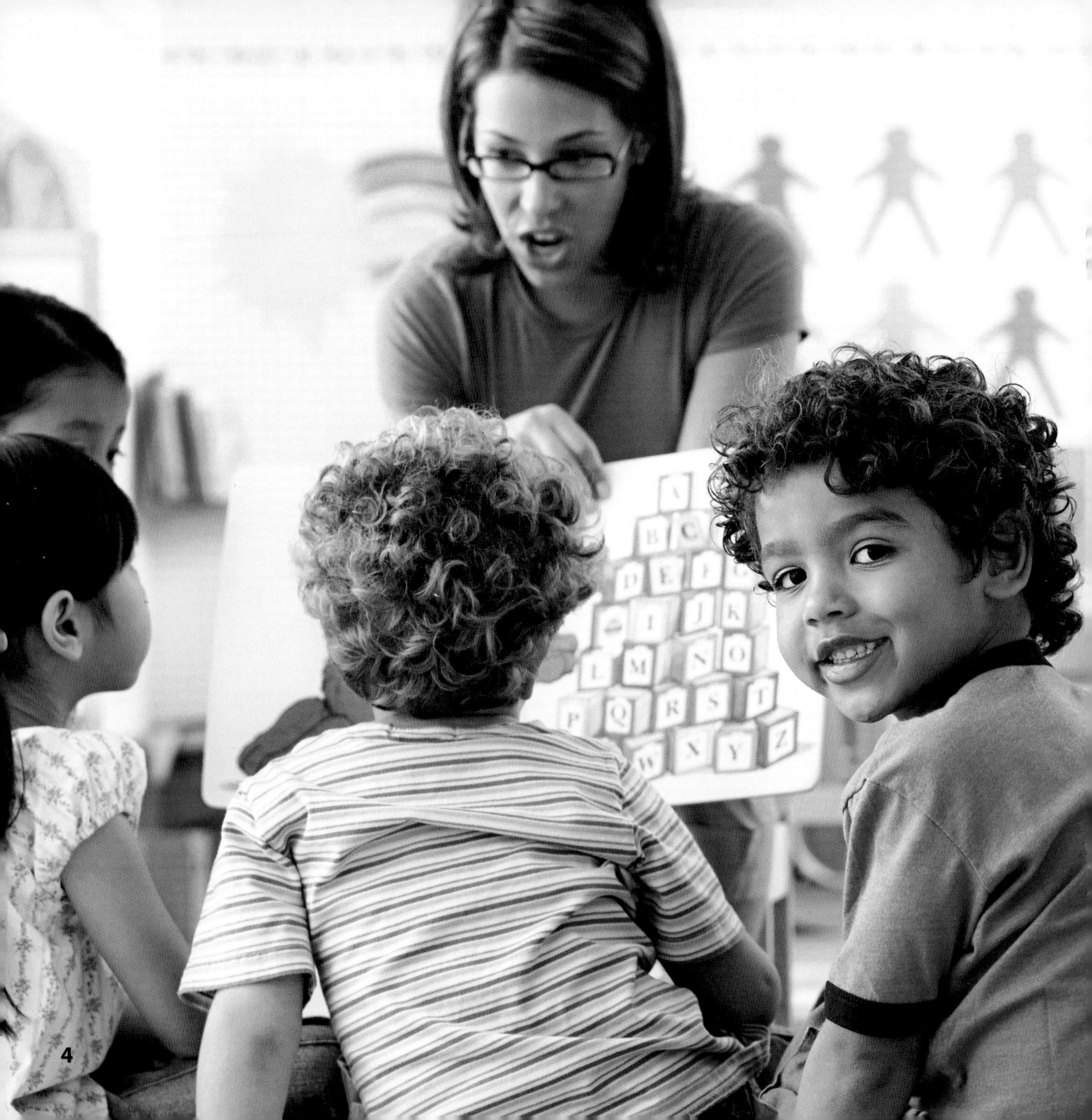

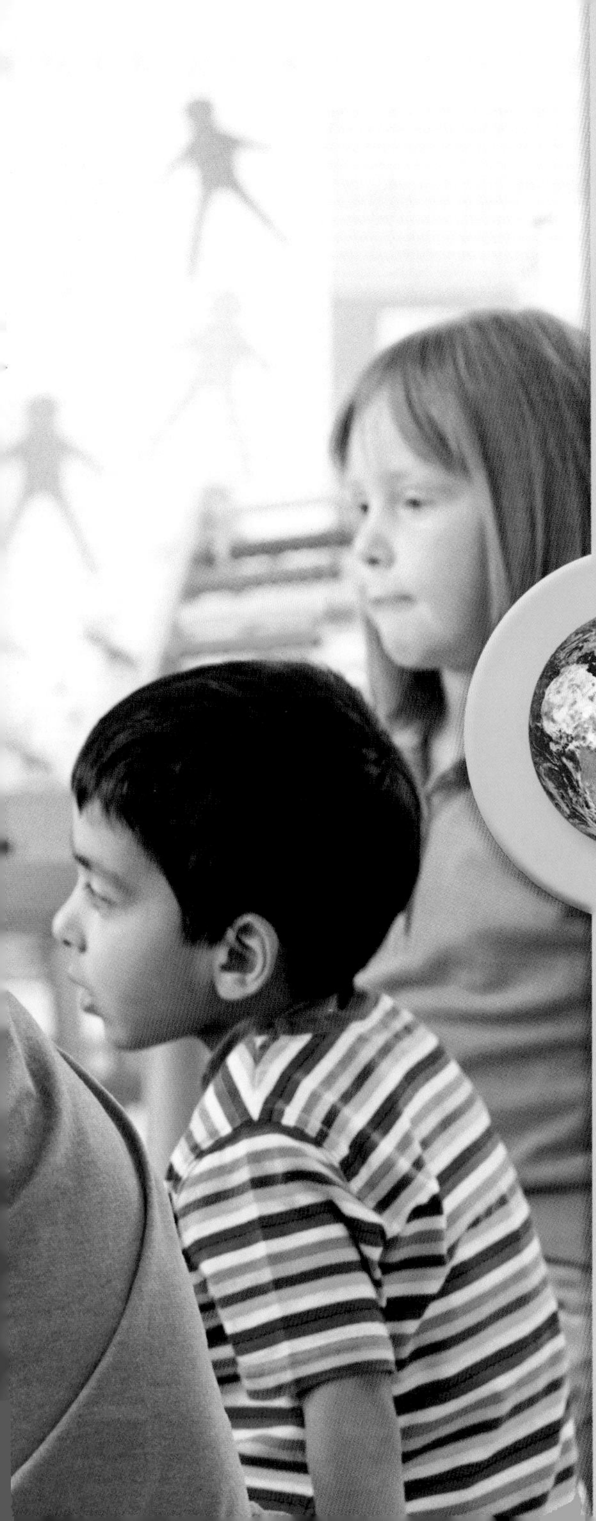

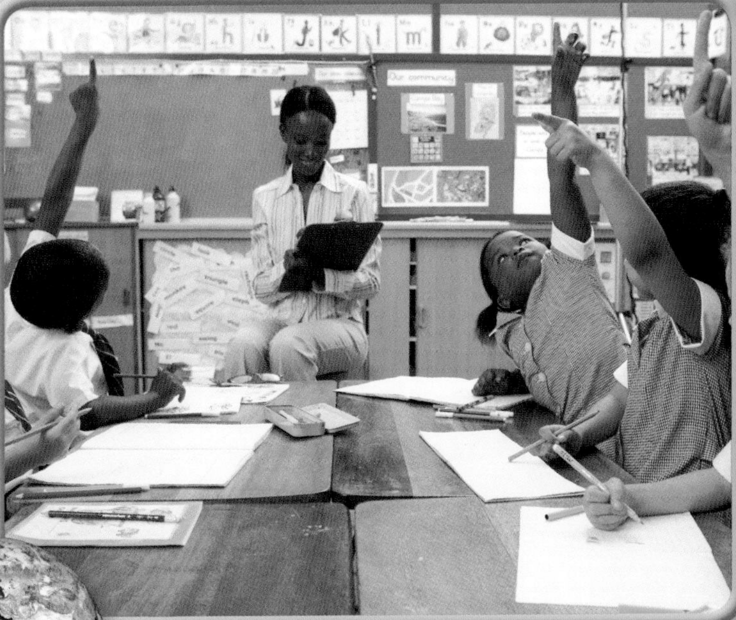

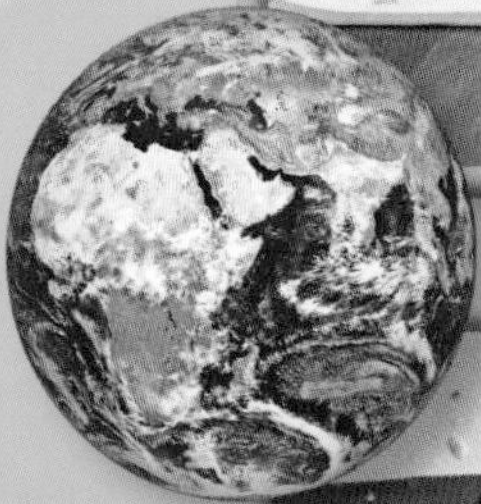

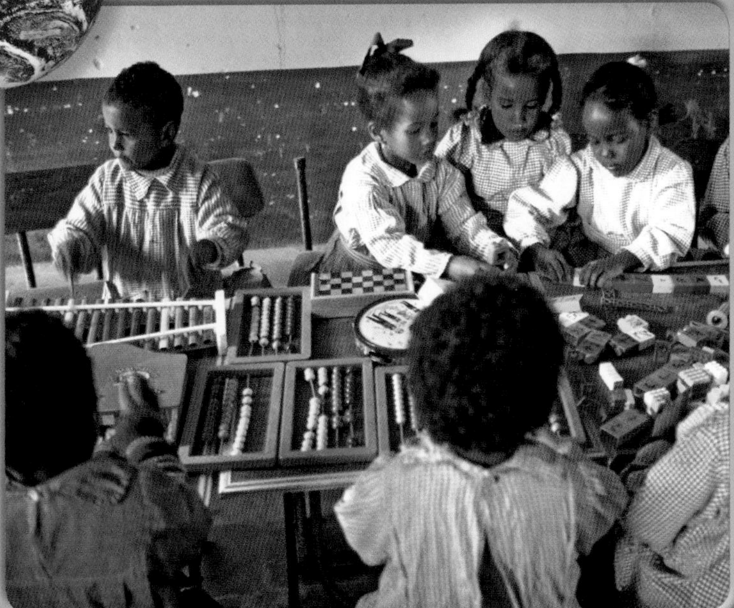

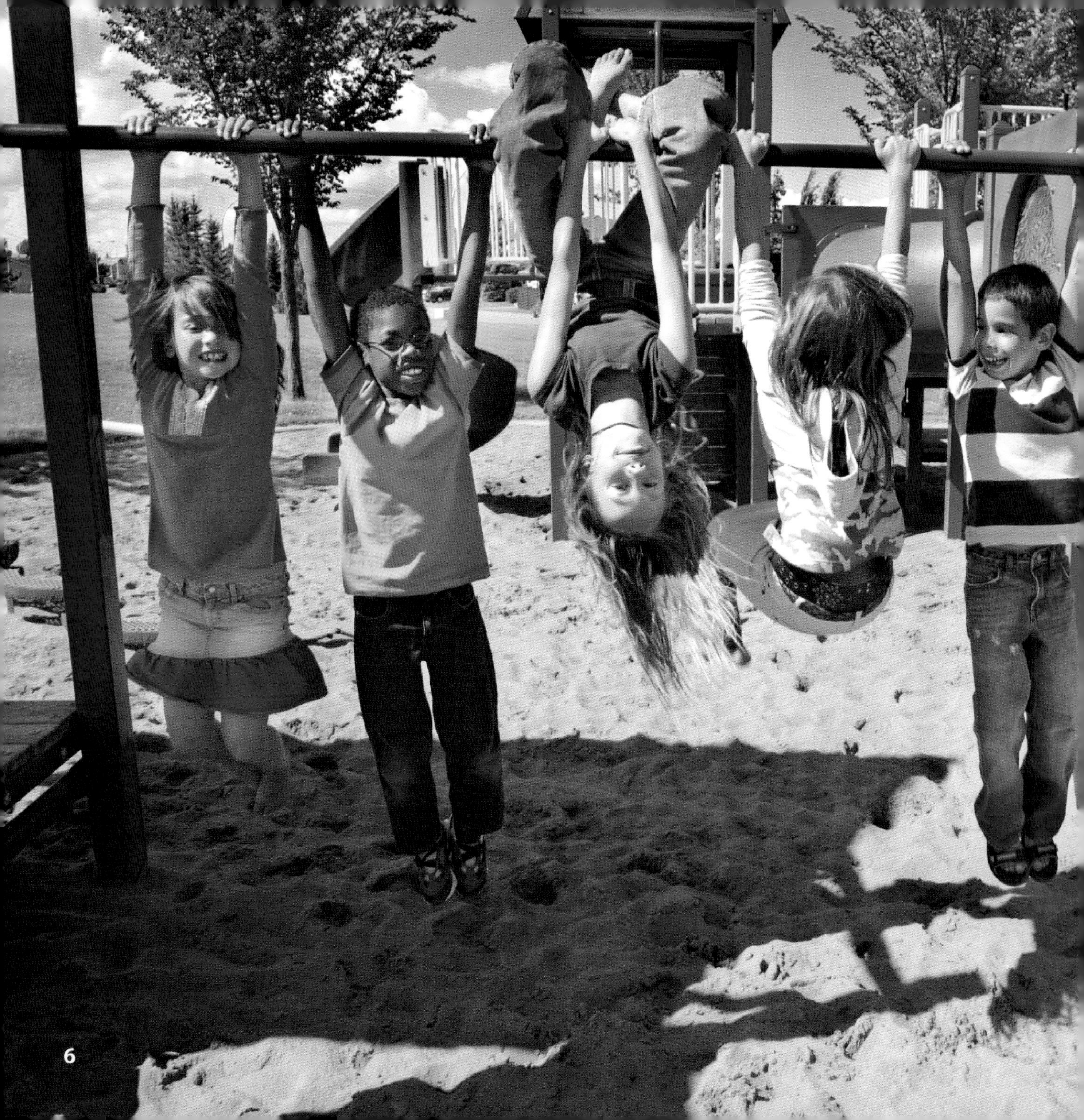

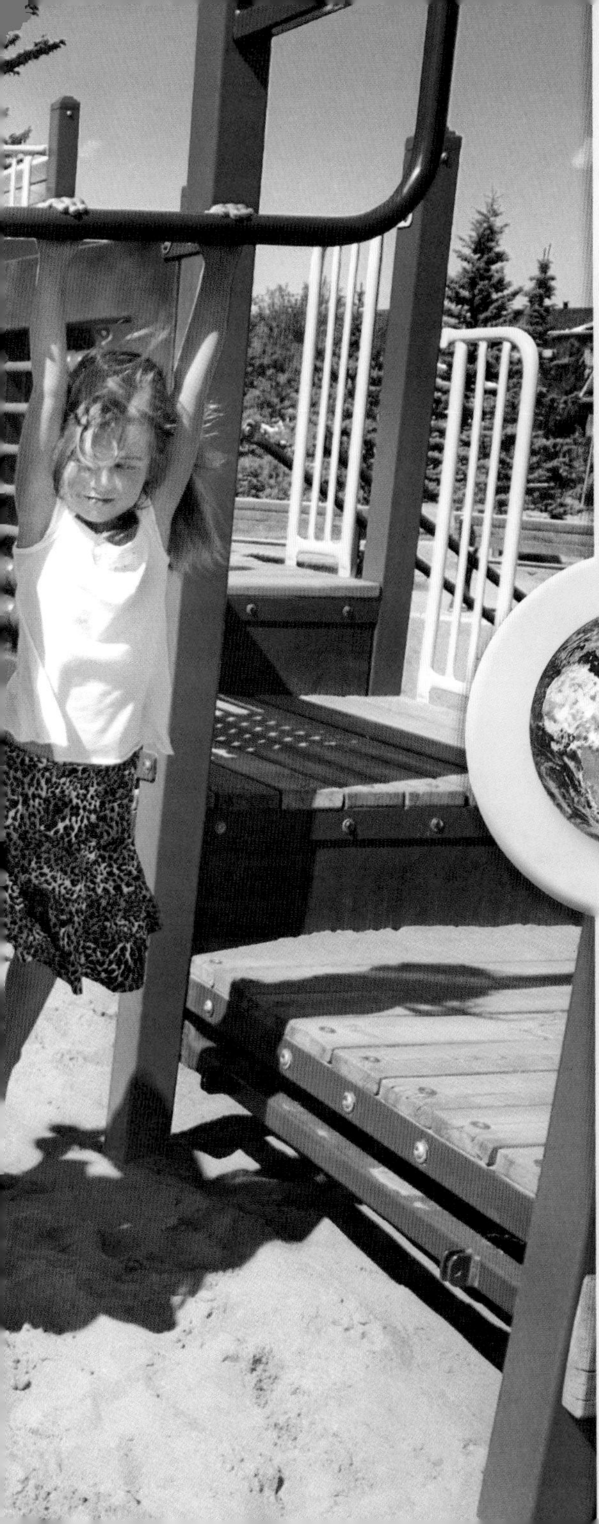

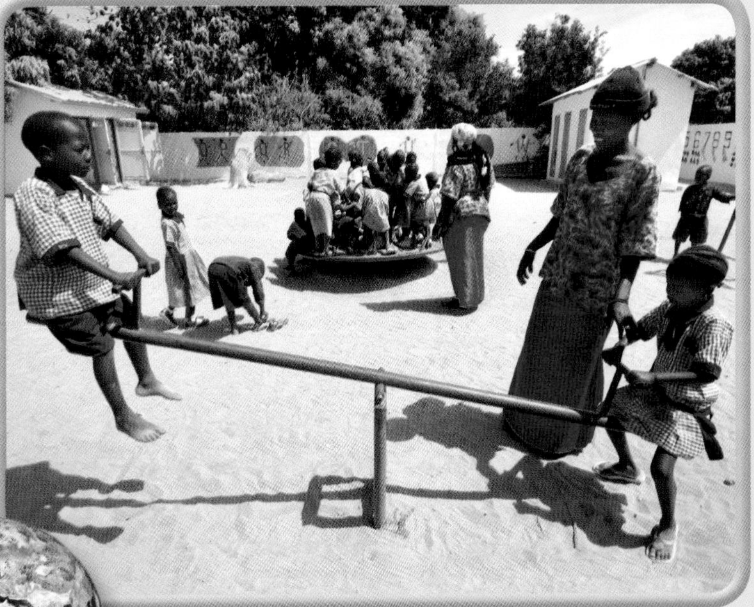

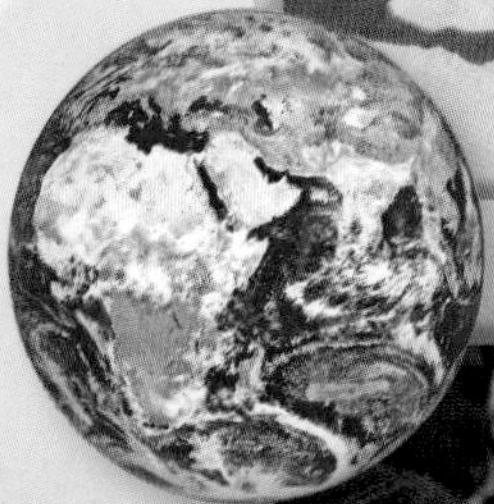

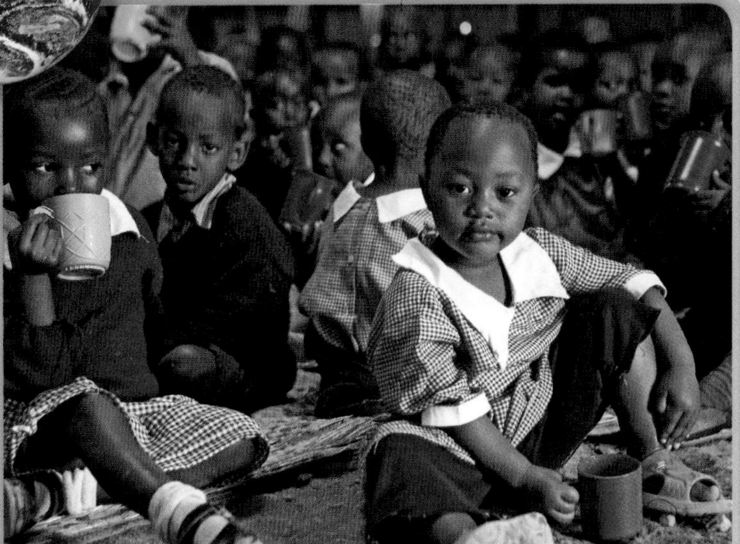

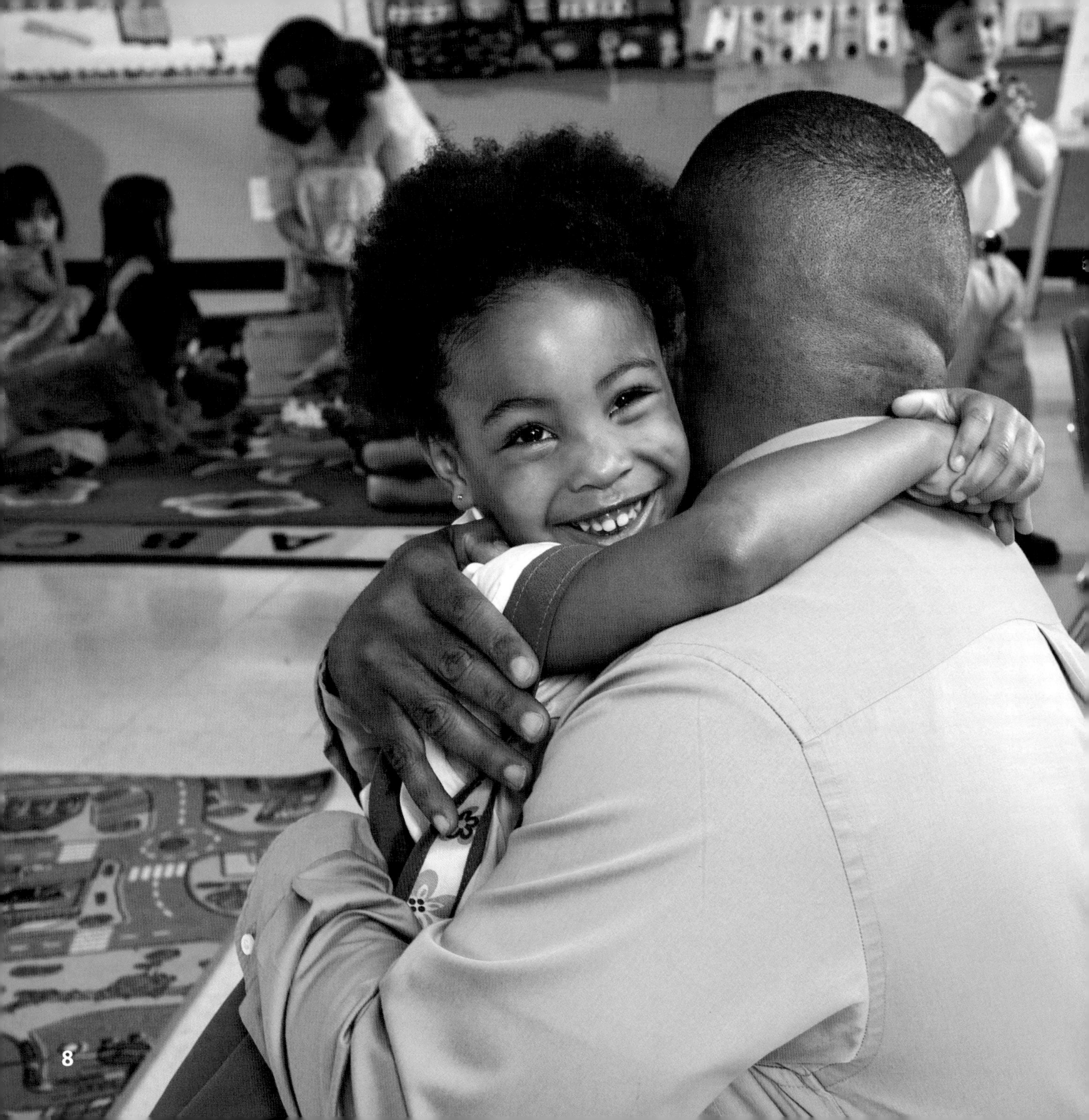